SEX AND THE SINGLE CHURCH SISTER

HOW TO KEEP YOUR DRESS **ON** WHEN YOU WANT TO TAKE IT **OFF**

SHÁ GIVENS

I CAN FLY PUBLISHING
LOS ANGELES, CALIFORNIA

All rights reserved.
Copyright © 2010 by Shá Givens
Some names have been altered to protect the identity of
real individuals. No part of this book may be reproduced
or transmitted in any form or by any means without
permission in writing from the publisher.

ISBN: 978- 0-970-98417-3

Published by:
I CAN FLY Publishing
P.O. Box 62010
Los Angeles, CA 90062 U.S.A

Scripture taken from the New King James Version
Copyright © 1979, 1980, 1982 by Thomas Nelson Inc.
Used by permission. All rights reserved.

Library of Congress Control Number: 2010937079

Printed in the United States of America

This book is dedicated to
CASSANDRA JOHNSON
A mighty warrior for the Kingdom of God. A young mother who refused to remain a statistic. I thank the Lord for allowing me to be your mentor. I am honored. Continue to stand in the midst of adversity when the challenges of life come your way. You have the power to soar like an eagle. Mount up with wings, I say. This is your time, this is your destiny!

Isaiah 40:31

CONTENTS

ACKNOWLEDGEMENTS
INTRODUCTION
A NOTE

HOME ALONE	1
RUNNING OUT OF STEEM	7
ROLLER COASTERS	13
CORN FLAKES	19
GIVING UP	25
CLOSET FREAKS	31
EMOTIONS	35
GOT HOPE?	39
PIECES	45
COOKIE COUPONS	49
SUGAR MOMMA	55
THAT'S MY HUSBAND	57
MR. PROPHECY	63
WHEN YOUR MAN IS THE DEVIL	67
WOLF ALERT	73
DIRT & BONES	77
SPIRITUAL DETOXIFICATION	81
INVISIBLE LINES	85
IS THE FAT LADY SINGING?	91
A DREAM	99
I AM	105

ACKNOWLEDGMENTS

Words cannot adequately express my gratitude for each of you. Your support, prayers and contributions have helped me in ways I could not have done alone. Please know how special you are to me. The Lord craftily placed you in my life for a purpose. Living the single life has been a task in itself. Most of you know my story. Without your love and unwavering support; I may not be the woman that I am today. You are the shoulders I stand on. Thank you for believing in the Single Church Sister vision:

Deidra Reid
Rachelle Guillory
Imani Hayward
Darla Givens
Bobbie Givens
Lisa Humphrey
Rev. Tanis Matthews
Rev. Angela Giles
Rev. Tosha Freeman
Tammy Carpenter
Elease Wallace
Lenora Brown
Maynard Matthews

INTRODUCTION

Over the years I've had plenty of time to reflect on my past and when my issues began. I remember it as if it were yesterday. With one eye open I took my first peek at an X-Rated film blaring on a cable television late night movie channel. I was only seven years old. It was three months before my eighth birthday. This was the beginning of a downfall. I didn't see it coming. I was still a child, just curious like most kids at that age. Something happened that day I regretted for years. My innocence was shattered by one image; that affected my life for the next twenty years. Spending time in abortion clinics, doctor's offices, sneaking pregnancy tests home, hoping no one would find out my secret was not the way I wanted to live. Once I tasted the forbidden fruit, I couldn't turn back. I became one of those girls who always had to have a man. I can't remember ever being alone back in those days. My college girlfriends would often ask, "Have you ever been without a man?" "No", I replied. Like any drug addict who craves the next high or a food fanatic that can't turn down a plate of food, I always had to have a man on my arm. I couldn't imagine life any other way.

Through the years I've paid dearly for my need to fulfill the chase. After I accepted Jesus Christ into my life "for real" fourteen years ago, I found myself finally alone. It was the first time in a long time my telephone wasn't ringing and no one was calling with an invitation to dinner. I was so ready for a change because I was now tired. Tired of being in control of my own destiny and messing it up. Running from God had worn me out. I didn't realize how exhausted I was until I actually stopped running. I vividly remember walking down the red carpeted aisle in church during the altar call to make my public confession for Jesus Christ. It was August 1996. I took a long deep breath and stood in front of the altar. I didn't care how many people stared. As far as I was concerned none of those people had a hell to throw me in or a heaven to accept me into. I was just fine. Jesus and I were on a new mission.

I came home that afternoon and had a long talk with the Lord. I promised to serve Him, live Holy, and be obedient. I also reminded Him of my sexual need since I was accustomed to having a man. I assumed He would bless me with a husband within a year. I made a point to attend Bible study each week, read the Word of God, pray, and serve in the church. I was determined to get emotionally healed and delivered from all of life's past drama. After all, I believed my husband would show up within a year and I wanted to be ready for him. As you can see that was my own plan. Fourteen years have passed and I am still a Single Church Sister…

A NOTE

A REAL TALK ABOUT FAITH, LIVING SINGLE AND THE STRUGGLE

If we don't confront pertinent issues such as sex, living single and how it fits into our faith, we will continue to deceive ourselves. It is important for each of us to acknowledge where we are in regards to our sexuality and faith in order to move forward. I will attempt to be as candid as possible without offending anyone. Moreover, if you are offended then hear my heart; offending you is not my intention. I solely seek to bring light, freedom, exposure and breakthrough for many women who need a change, a new beginning and deliverance in this area. Allow us this without ridicule or judgment. If the desire for sex, marriage and intimacy is not an issue for you, then please, pray earnestly for the millions of women who are struggling. God Bless!

HOME ALONE

Whoever said loneliness is a state of mind and it's easy to remedy—LIED. If you're single, divorced, widowed, or unhappily married and struggling, you may have heard this phrase, "Stop tripping, keep busy and the loneliness will fade away!" They just don't understand. Stop tripping? Keep busy? We are busy, but it doesn't always change the way we feel.

If you've ever heard this statement or something similar, you can raise your hand with the rest of us and say, "AMEN!" The phrase sounds more like "Get over it, silly!" These words are insensitive and un-thoughtful, but people utter such statements to single folks as if they have total control over the periodic emotion. Like most of us, you probably grit your teeth, smile and pretend you're not fazed when you hear it. We all have a tendency to politely shrug things off even when they hurt. You may even assume there is something wrong with you for feeling this way. I am here to tell you—you are not alone. Loneliness is not an easy topic to discuss. You run the risk of being perceived as desperate, ungrateful or dissatisfied with God.

Most single church sisters in the twenty-first century are busier than ever. Think about it. We do everything possible to stay active and keep our minds out of the gutter. We feed the homeless. Sing in the church choir and save the whales, just to name a few. Yet we can still find ourselves struggling with the reality that we're single and alone. Loneliness has a way of rearing its ugly little head when we are doing our best to avoid it.

HIDING BEHIND YOUR WORK?

It's easy to create a shield of protection from loneliness. The most common protector for the ambitious single sister is her career. Do you add additional hours to your work schedule than required? Are you emotionally driven by climbing the ladder of success because of an unfulfilled void in your personal life? Many times these thoughts and actions are birthed from a deep hidden feeling of loneliness. Work is the perfect mask. It can drastically reduce the reality that loneliness exists. Of course we rarely admit it because it's embarrassing to openly agree, but let's take a moment and think. Being busy in the office makes it easier to forget about Mr. Right, at least for a few hours. Moreover, at the end of the work day our minds often revert back to what we're missing—companionship.

Let's be frank, most of us desire someone to come home to at night. After a challenging day, we want that special someone to make us feel as if everything is going to be alright. Being held in your honey's arms has a way of erasing every nerve-racking word your boss spoke. The thought of a big hug and a tantalizing dinner after work sounds intoxicating. The reality is, there is no honey waiting for you when you return home, and your dinner is frozen in the freezer. For now, it's easier to hide behind your career than focus on what you don't have.

THE DATING GAME

Have you fallen for a man who refuses to commit? Does he make every excuse not to settle down with you? Is he more interested in climbing the ladder of success than spending time with you? If you ask for more time and attention does he reply, "Let's take things slow." Sister, taking things slow can be a good thing, but sometimes our definitions differ. His slow can mean have sex and commit later. Your slow might mean commit now and have sex after the wedding. Ouch! You're living on two different planets. Pluto and earth are millions of miles apart. It's awkward. One of you will end up letting go or giving in. Don't let the one who gives in be you.

Let's face it—it's frustrating wanting someone whose feelings are not mutual. I'm sure we've all been there.

But, it's easier being alone than a victim of one sided love. Being hurt and disappointed repeatedly can escalate your loneliness to an all time high. Loneliness and disappointment are a bad combination. I know we all hope our Mr. Right Now will change, but we must preserve our peace of mind in the interim. Be fair to yourself. Unfortunately, you are dating someone that still makes you feel lonely. His infrequent pop-ups can many times leave you feeling lonelier than you were before he arrived. Your special someone is either too busy or uninterested in the relationship. You're hanging in there hoping things will change soon. After all, you believe it's better to hope he'll come around than let him go.

WHEN ARE YOU GETTING MARRIED?

If you've heard this question a million times, don't raise your hand. It's a very common question for women in their thirties, forties and even fifties. The older you get, the more you will hear it. Most of the time these words are uttered from the mouths of our parents, siblings, co-workers and a few not so close friends who don't have a clue what's going on in your world. They see you from a distance and wonder why you're still single. After all, you're talented, educated and skilled with every strand of hair on your head in its proper place. You look good, dress like an "A" list celebrity and seem like the perfect match for some eligible bachelor. It makes sense for them to wonder why you're still single, but unfortunately you can't respond to a question you don't have the answer to. You're still trying to figure out why you're single also.

SINGLE AGAIN
I'm sure you're still in shock. You can't believe it. This time around you're single with kids and a desk piled high with overdue bills you can't pay. Your favorite scripture is pinned to your refrigerator door that says, *(Philippians 4:13) "I can do all things through Christ who strengthens me."* The divorce almost took the wind out of you. You were married for several years and dedicated your entire life to your marriage. For matters unknown whether it was your fault or your ex-husband's, you're back at the place you vowed never to return—single life, the rat race. You remember it vividly. You dated every Tom, Derrick and Larry hoping one of them would be—THE ONE. It was a full time job. And here you are, inducted back into the sorority of single sisters.

A WORD FROM THE WISE
Feelings of loneliness, low self-esteem, and financial uncertainty can send your mind on a helicopter ride after divorce. While all of these unwanted issues parade themselves during this strange and unfamiliar season, you must keep your sister friend circle close—support is key. Some church sisters have been known to go out and find the first man on the street to fulfill a sexual and emotional void after divorce. Yes, it's lonely, unfamiliar, and uncomfortable and you're still mad at the way it all happened. Sister, please take note: a temporary seat-filler will not heal your wounds or fulfill your need for revenge. Sex with a complete stranger or the guy at the local department store who flirted with you all those years while you were married cannot remove your hurt. Instant gratification has long term

affects that can set you further back than you already feel. Hold on tight to God's promises. Let Him vindicate you if you've been mistreated. The Lord hasn't left you. Allow yourself time to grieve the severed relationship. Let God's healing power engulf your very being. He will help you through this difficult season. Keep your dress on and trust God.

RUNNING OUT OF STEEM

You can easily throw yourself a private pity-party when reality hits. No prince charming, frogs or potential suitors are knocking the front door down to meet you. The only people dialing your telephone number are your best girlfriends and a select bill collector from an old credit card company you couldn't pay. You're trying to figure why. Am I too fat? Skinny? Is my hair too short? Why doesn't anybody want me? You can't help but ask these questions since no man or the right man has taken any real interest in you.

When the opposite sex doesn't seem to notice we're alive, we begin examining ourselves to see if something is wrong. We compare every detail of our bodies, clothes and hair to other females passing down aisle five at the supermarket. We can only see our flaws and highlight her assets. The silence in our personal lives has officially taken its toll. We're close to hitting rock bottom in the self-esteem department. We clearly notice it fading away but we're not quite sure how to get it back.

There may have been a time in your life when you felt like the hottest thing around. In this season, your condition looks completely different. You feel far away from hot on a good day. Someone in your office may give you a compliment on your favorite pair of paten leather shoes or the brand new zebra print handbag you purchased for your birthday. It's nice to know you've got great taste, but you're still thinking, "What about me?" You don't feel beautiful anymore. Hair extensions, make-up, eyelashes, or a new tummy-tuck doesn't boost your self-esteem level. Your state of singleness makes you think you're missing it in the beauty department.

MY STORY: A LOOK IN THE MIRROR
Every now and then I find myself in a fight. As if someone were trying to steal my self-esteem, I'm holding on to it for dear life. Fifty questions run through my mind, "Is my waist too large? Should I lose ten extra pounds? What should I do with my hair? Eyebrows? Puffy cheeks?" Finally, I had to say, "ENOUGH" and mean it for a change. All of my hang ups in regards to size, outer appearance and sex appeal became overwhelming.

As a child, my sister Darla was considered the fine one in the family. I was the cute one but I wanted to be fine too. I loved my big sister but I couldn't figure out, "What made her so gorgeous?" A bigger butt? Larger breasts? What? Finally, during my sophomore year in High School I took my cute and worked it to my advantage. I identified my assets and extenuated each one. Everything from my small frame, outgoing personality, and artistic talent were used to remind me how special I was. There was no one else in the world created exactly like me. I began to appreciate who I was as a package and not focus so much on what I considered a flaw. I knew God didn't make a mistake when He handcrafted every detail of my being inside and out. I was wonderfully and beautifully made. *(Psalm 139:14)"I will praise You, for I am fearfully and wonderfully made."*

• • •

A DOSE OF TRUTH

Comparing ourselves to magazine cover models and Hollywood celebrities is unrealistic and unfair. Our famous female counterparts don't look like their very own pictures after the graphics department finished airbrushing the wrinkles, blending the blemishes and covering up the forehead lines. So, why should we continue comparing ourselves to false images?

Sisters, we can embrace beauty, but not at the price of our peace of mind and financial well-being. Keeping up with the Jones' in regards to outward appearance is a race we will never win. There will always be someone prettier, with a bigger butt, faster car, and more talent than you and I put together. Moreover, you are uniquely made in God's image and there is no other replica on this earth like you. We must envision ourselves the same way God sees us. All of our assets were given by God to create a unique package. Of course we all have something on our bodies we would like to change, clip, cut off, or wish away into the corn fields. Who doesn't? For some of us it may be sagging breasts, a bloated stomach or a double dose of cellulite on your upper thighs. Nevertheless, it is our duty to celebrate our assets and not focus on the liabilities.

We all want to feel loved, appreciated and beautiful, but we must love ourselves first in order to experience true love with a man. When we don't love ourselves as we should, we are bound for trouble. Our quest for love while stationed in the low-self esteem zone is dangerous. Here are two examples:

ATTENTION GETTERS
Showing large portions of skin and breasts to appeal to the opposite sex is the most common attention getter. It is a for sure way to make a man notice you. Let's be honest. It feels good to hear a compliment or gain someone's interest. Most women enjoy hearing how beautiful they are. Flattery is the fastest way to boost someone's self-esteem especially when it's low. Nevertheless, all attention is not good attention. A potential suitor should find true beauty in your spirit, natural appeal, and personality. Leave your physical assets to a man's imagination. Attention based solely on sex appeal and exposed body parts is risky. When a man is only interested in a woman's physical attributes she should always question his motives. Falling for a man

with purely physical intentions can lead you straight into a sex trap. You can wake up one morning not knowing what hit you. Sister, keep your dress on and run. You will save yourself from a lifetime full of heartache.

NO LIMITS

Deficient self-esteem will attempt to rob you from understanding who you are and whose you are. Compromise will creep into your thought life. You'll find yourself kicking your morals and spiritual beliefs to the curb in order to please your new man. Doing whatever it takes to keep him around becomes a priority, even if it means watering down your belief system. After all, you don't want to lose him. You're afraid this may be your last chance at love and a long term relationship. You convince yourself its okay to take your dress off although your spirit is screaming the exact opposite, *"No, wait!"* A part of you believes the sexual relationship is the only asset you possess to keep him. You begin offering yourself in ways you never imagined. However he wants it, three-some, four-some, anything-goes-some. At the end of the day, you won't know who you are anymore.

GETTING YOUR STEEM BACK

If you feel as if you're running out of self-esteem, do a self check. Find five great things you like about yourself. If you can't think of any, ask family and friends. Speak life, hope and thanksgiving about every situation you find yourself in. Find the brighter side of everything. Encourage yourself daily. Celebrate you. Be grateful for your hair type, eyes, nose and your beautiful skin. Thank God for your kind and compassionate spirit. Ask Him to show you how special you are.

FIVE WAYS TO INCREASE YOUR SELF-ESTEEM

- Do not receive any negative words spoken
- Find Biblical scriptures that offer hope and healing
- Surround yourself with people who celebrate you
- Believe in yourself in spite of how you feel at times
- Speak life and counter every lie with God's truth

ROLLER COASTERS

The best part of any roller coaster ride is getting on in the beginning. Whoo-hoo! Your hair is standing on top of your head and the wind gives you little mercy. Anticipation mixed with the fear of the unknown is a thrill. After you've fastened your seat belt, took a deep breath and exhaled, off you go—skies the limit. It's not until the middle of the ride when you reach an unexpected loop that makes your stomach drop twenty feet, you find yourself yelling, *"Get me off!"* The ride is uncomfortable and scary.

Roller coasters can be a lot like a brand new relationship. You cannot discern if your potential mate wants to be in a committed relationship or if he's in it simply for the ride. For most women, it doesn't take us long to figure out if we want the man or not. After a few in-depth telephone conversations and a night on the town we usually know if he's a keeper. Your radar button will sound off immediately.

Under normal circumstances a man doesn't have to figure out if you want him or not, most of us make it clear by our actions. If you're the domestic type, you'll want to prepare him a meal and show off your cooking skills. You quickly start thinking up all the ways in which you can make him happy. Our nurturing ways and ability to go beyond the call of duty in the beginning of a relationship speaks for itself.

STREET LIGHTS
If I could personally shake the hands of Garrett Morgan and thank him for inventing the stop light, I would. Trust me; he did all of us a huge favor. Street lights are signals designed to keep order while drivers are traveling on a journey. Like any common driver bound toward a destination, church sisters should likewise be attempting to fulfill our God ordained assignments by traveling on a purpose filled path . Furthermore, signals are also given to keep us on track and avoid accidents. Fender benders, scrapes, aches, pain and even death can be avoided when we follow the signals. They exist to protect everyone on the road.

Have you ever dated a man who set off negative warning signals the first time you met him? Your spirit was uncomfortable and uneasy. Something was not right but you had no tangible evidence to support your case. You may have even ignored the alarm thinking you were being paranoid and over cautious. Months later, you found yourself mixed up in a spider web of one-sided love. You're in love with him but the feelings are not mutual. He wasn't one of the bad guys. He's a good guy who just isn't God's guy. Your strong sense of *"no"* or *"go"* were on their job. After the relationship hit a snag you were reminded of the alarm you sensed in the beginning. Your personal signal system was always there to protect you.

Three basic types of signals include:
1) Signals you can visibly see (eye-gate)
2) Signs you can hear (ear-gate)
3) Warnings you can feel (feel-gate)

We serve such a great God. He never leaves us without warning when danger is ahead. Signals that are ear-gate and eye-gate are the most obvious. For instance, if you've been in a relationship for a few months or more and your man refuses to allow you to answer the telephone or drop by his house without calling on occasion, it's time to raise your feminine antennas. Please note; there are exceptions to some rules but don't always disregard his telephone hoarding as coincidental. Second example, if you're dating someone who walks away from you every time he answers the cell phone and likes to speak in riddles while you're around, consider it a warning.

Warnings you can feel will always affect you physically. Although every woman is different the most common physical warnings can include an uneasiness in your stomach or a lump in your throat when his name is mentioned or he comes around. If you're sleeping with this man, you can also feel as if you need to throw up, moments or days after you've had sex with him. Some may consider this warning sign extreme but its real and its happening to hundreds and thousands of women who sense the call of God on their lives. Such an extreme warning is used to get your undivided attention.

Most of women are extremely intuitive. Let's do ourselves a favor and not live in a state of denial anymore. We can save ourselves from a bundle of heartache and wasted time in the future. These signals are God's way of saying, *"This man is not for you!"* Sister, when you hear it, put your track shoes on and run. On your mark, get set, go...

The man God has for you will make you feel a sense of peace and purpose when he is in your presence. You can relax, relate and enjoy being yourself. Your signal system will not sound the alarm every time the telephone rings or he's talking to another woman after church. We serve a God of peace not confusion. *(1 Corinthians 14:33) "For God is not the author of confusion but of peace, as in all the churches of the saint."* God's man will add to the great woman you are not take away. The right man will not leave you questioning his every move.

PLAYERS

Can you name a single church sister who is content being one out of many women in a man's romantic life? Probably not. Most of us would prefer being the only one, but of course this is not always the case. If you are in a relationship and have the slightest notion you might be getting played, you probably are. It's a tough pill to swallow to think we're being used by someone we care about. Nonetheless, we must face the truth. Your mate may be skilled at sleeping with several women at the same time. The thought is unsettling, I know, but you do not have to be a victim of the playerhood. If you have any inkling you could be a victim of player-itus, put your track shoes on and run as fast as you can. Are you ready? On your mark, get set, go…

When God shows up in your love life He will send someone designed just for you. God's man will find satisfaction with you alone. Your man will arrive already delivered from any past playerhood tendencies. His previous struggle with player-itus will almost seem unfathomable after you appear on the scene. Will he ever get tempted? Yes, but he more than likely will not chase the first skirt that motions his way. You will not feel the need to scramble and check his cell phone messages when he runs outside to take out the garbage. Your spirit will be at peace. Your feminine antennas won't constantly remain on standby.

FRIENDS WITH BENEFITS

Benefit packages have become all too common in the lives of single sisters. Most of us know someone or have personally experienced a sexual relationship with a man who considers his lover "just-a-friend" and vice-versa. When we become comfortable calling a sexual partner "just-a-friend" something is wrong. Sharing our bodies with a man who doesn't think more of us than a friend speaks to our level of self-esteem and settling. There is usually no intention to make you his wife. True friends are people who love you and genuinely care about your well-being spiritually, emotionally and physically.

The definition of friends is taken out of context far too often. Friends are not people we should casually have sex with. The two don't mix unless it's under the covenant of marriage. God's plan for sex is best. Sex with a "friend" most often always taints the innocence of your platonic relationship. It will leave you wanting more. Perhaps a commitment, respect and love will become the forefront of your desires. The confusion and emotional stress of having sex with a "friend" can be overwhelming. Feelings of jealousy, awkwardness, and shame you hadn't felt before the sexual encounter will change the course of your friendship. Consider yourself worthy of deserving more.

CORN FLAKES

If you've ever been stood up, left with a dinner bill, or falsely promised a new and improved relationship and got nothing back in return, you have entered the corn flake zone. Flakey people do wacky things that can leave you feeling hurt and embarrassed. Corn flakes come in all sorts of packages. Tall, short, skinny, fat, young and old. They all have one thing in common. They rarely fulfill their promises. Of course we're all human and we make mistakes. Moreover, consistent flakiness with little to no remorse can seem unbearable when you're looking forward to a new friendship you thought had potential for more. A flakey potential mate can make you want to give up on love once and for all. You never know what he's going to do next. You're constantly trying to figure him out.

You have no idea where he's coming from in relation to you. If you dress up in your favorite outfit, only to find out hours later he's a no-show, you're heart-broken. Disappointment has knocked on your door once again. Having an attraction to someone who takes your feelings lightly can launch you into pity-party mode.

As women we tend to hold onto hope until the very end. We want the man we care about to change. Once we've identified a measure of potential we consider him instantly redeemable. Our minds get fixated on the notion that we can motivate him to become a better person. We spend countless hours worrying and wanting our potential mate to convert into a trustworthy beau when he has no desire to do so. He doesn't think there is a serious problem. His flakiness is shrugged off as a slight character flaw that should be tolerated or ignored. The blessing in knowing you're dating a corn flake is simple. You found out he's a flake before the relationship could become serious.

MY STORY: THE CORN FLAKE ZONE

In the late 1990's, I met one of the most amazing men ever. He reminded me of a magazine bachelor centerfold. Professional, handsome, goal driven, and he loved God. A friend introduced us at a celebrity basketball game in Los Angeles one summer. I'd been walking faithfully with the Lord for a while and was looking forward to meeting new people with the potential of dating. After Brock and I met we immediately hit it off. Our conversations, goals, and ideologies were all in sync. He loved having dinner at Sushi restaurants or his favorite spot in Marina Del Rey. Paying the bill or treating me like a lady wasn't his issue. Keeping his word was a challenge. After he'd drop me off we would often hug and say good night. *"I'll call you tomorrow", he'd say.* I couldn't wait to get home from work and listen to the voice mail message. His voice was intoxicating. My finger was ready to push the repeat button. I could listen to his voice over and over again. After I pressed the play button there were zero messages left on the answering machine. He never called. Hours went by and nothing. I woke up the next morning and assumed he got busy at work and couldn't call. I was certain I would hear from him the next day. Finally two weeks passed and the phone rang. It was Brock. He spoke as if nothing happened. He claimed he'd been busy at the office. I wasn't quite sure how to respond. Was this his usual character? Can I trust him not to disappear again? I asked myself all these questions and continued caring for him in hopes that he would fall in love with me. I was sure he'd find time in between his hectic schedule to pick up the phone and call if he cared for me like I did him.

We continued to date on a regular basis. I pretended his flakiness would eventually work itself out. His unfulfilled telephone calls or cancelled dates were annoying but I blamed it on the fact that this is a goal driven man, therefore he needs time and energy to secure his future. After holding on to hope that he would one day treat me like a priority and not an after thought—I got tired. I prayed and asked God, *"Is he the one?"* There was no answer. Soon after, Brock expressed his desire to take our relationship to another level and make it exclusive. I was happy. I didn't want anybody else anyway. Finally, we were getting somewhere. He left my apartment that evening and I thanked God for allowing him to see what a great catch I was. The next evening Brock returned after a long day at work and asked me to sit down. It sounded serious. I was nervous. He claimed he couldn't move forward with the exclusive relationship after all because he's still not ready. I was emotionally worn out by that point. Being wishy-washy and back and forth with my emotions had gone far enough. I had to mentally release him and hand the whole situation over to God. I couldn't change this man. His issues were deeper than anything I could handle. I couldn't see him again. So I walked away from the Corn Flake Zone.

• • •

Flakey people will always leave you on the edge of your seat. You'll never know what's going to happen next. Playing the wild card with a flakey potential mate is unhealthy and unbalanced. It can leave you mentally stressed out. You'll always wonder when and if your special corn flake will turn his life around and come through for you.

In order to protect your heart, turn your flakey mate issues over to God. Believe that God can change, heal and deliver him, but don't ponder on the issue at the expense of your own emotional wellbeing. God needs you in position for the great purpose and destiny He has in store for you. Do not let your special corn flake distract you from your God ordained journey. The Lord has you and your special corn flake in the palm of His hand. Let go and give it to the Master.

FIVE WAYS TO DETECT A POTENTIAL CORNFLAKE

- Rarely calls, leaving you responsible for calling
- Doesn't call or text when running late or can't show up
- Expects you to pay for dinner and outings most of the time
- Always prefers staying home instead of taking you out
- Stares at other women in your presence

GIVING UP

If you feel like picking up the telephone to feel the touch, caress and love from that unforgettable ex-boyfriend who made you feel like you were on top of the world—WAIT! Your obedience to wait on God in regards to your sex life is not in vain. I know it's been several years or months since you've been intimate with a man, but you've come too far to turn back now. Yes, you're struggling with the overwhelming urge to be intimate with a man. Sometimes your desires rage out of control. You are not quite sure how much longer you can hang on without the love and passion you deeply desire. Celibacy seems like an impossible feat, but hold on, help is on the way.

HOT AND BOTHERED

The flesh battle is probably the most rigorous duel in the lives of single men and women. Some believe it's unnatural for a single Christian woman to desire sexual intimacy. In other words, if she loves Jesus, she should never feel hot, bothered and ready to take her dress off. This particular mind-set implies that she is lose, fast, and spiritually immature if she struggles with the notion. The reality is, God created us as sexual beings with basic desires for intimacy. Nonetheless, God's ordained order of things requires these desires be satisfied in marriage only, although the feelings exist before marriage. *(Song of Solomon 3:5) "I charge you, O daughters of Jerusalem, by the gazelles or by the does of the field, do not stir up nor awaken love until it pleases."*

Living single for long periods of time can complicate a natural need. *(1 Corinthians 7:9) "But if they cannot exercise self-control, let them marry. For it is better to marry than to burn with passion."* Let's be honest. Many single church sisters are burning, yet there is no relief. Here is the dilemma; you're walking through life with a host of natural desires that are not being spiritually fulfilled. You were designed for intimacy yet you have no husband to supply the demand. The conflict arises because the two are not in sync. You are left with two options: 1) Wait on God to fulfill your desires spiritually (marriage). 2) Attempt to satisfy your own sexual desires with a non-husband, which is out of the will of God. (fornication/adultery). *(1Thessalonians 4:3)"For this is the will of God, your sanctification; that you should abstain from sexual immorality."*

Until the day your mate appears, it's pertinent to remain prayed up and consistently feeding on God's word. He will strengthen you and nourish your areas of weakness in times of need. Your spiritual exercise plan is critical for your sexual preservation. God's plan for sex in marriage is perfect. The repercussions of stepping outside of the will of God are treacherous. There is rarely a happy ending. I'm sure we can all recall a few horror stories attached to premarital sexual encounters. Think about it. After the sex ended, whether it lasted for two hours or three minutes you were left feeling unfulfilled afterwards. The reason is simple. The sexual experience was performed outside of God's will. Although you may have physically enjoyed it, the emotional consequences that you deal with afterwards whether immediate or months later are real. Sex outside of marriage most often leaves us wondering, will he stay or will he soon move on. We can feel a sense of shame and guilt after the love-making session filled with tricks and gymnastics ends without a glimmer of hope for a future.

WHEN YOU'RE NOT STRONG
The Creator is always looking out for our best interest. He sees our struggle. He knows our flesh burns at times. He has a plan. Although our sexual fulfillment may not come in the timing or manner in which we'd like, the Lord will give us a way of escape.

Fellowship is vital to your survival while abstaining from sex. Every woman should have a trustworthy sister circle she can be totally transparent with after the church lights go out. Please note: Your inner circle should be traveling on the same spiritual journey as you are. In other words, when you're feeling weak and vulnerable, your friends who sleep around, live with their boyfriends or think your abstinence campaign is a hoax, should not be the people you call for support. They cannot relate, at least not in their present state. Remember, you should reach out to sister friends who can encourage you, pray you through or even drive to your house when you're close to dialing your ex- boyfriend's telephone number.

ACCOUNTABILITY

First, pray and ask the Lord to send you an accountability partner. Allowing God to divinely place her in your life will weed out the people who mean you no good. You will avoid unnecessary drama and judgment. Once you've connected, let your sister friend know exactly what is happening with you during your time of struggle. Do not be afraid of their reaction and don't leave out any details. You will be surprised how much healing will manifest from a mere confession of sexual struggle. Your accountability partner will walk with you through your times of weakness and keep you spiritually lifted. Tell her what you're feeling and thinking. Be honest about your frustration. Releasing your thoughts and praying together will give you a sense of comfort and peace.

FIVE THINGS TO DO WHEN YOU FEEL LIKE GIVING UP

- Do not make decisions based on how you feel
- Create a small sister friend network for encouragement
- Avoid ex-lovers and men you are physically attracted to
- Read a scripture(s) each day that offer hope and healing
- Pray for the ability to overcome temptation

CLOSET FREAKS

How can you recognize a closet freak? Keep your eyes wide open and watch. A modern day closet freak can be male or female. They attend church most Sundays. Speak the latest church lingo and clap their hands during praise and worship; but as soon as the church lights go out, they're as wild as a hip-hop video star. Any flirtatious attention from someone in the pews gives them a thrill. The possibility of turning out a fellow church member in the bedroom feeds their ego, sex-drive and self-esteem. They are living double lives. A closet freak can listen to a powerful sermon that challenges their reckless behavior, shrug it off, and go right back to the drama after the benediction. They didn't feel a thing. Why? Their freaky behavior has desensitized any sense of conviction.

Moreover, there are other closet freaks who do feel convicted on occasion. They can experience shame and guilt immediately after a sexual encounter, but are unable to break the habit. They are addicted to sex. It is always at the forefront of their minds. An innocent conversation, topic or compliment can easily be turned into a subtle sexual advance or proposal.

FREAKY RECOVERY

If you think you're a closet freak, there is hope. Most spiritual and secular recovery programs begin by first acknowledging there is a problem. This is a good thing. Some habits are more difficult to break than others, but if you truly seek change, recovery is possible. Admitting you're an addict is key. This is a fundamental step to breaking the stronghold. Sometimes we can live a certain lifestyle for so long we can't imagine life differently. The enemy will make it seem as though your sexual appetite can never be satisfied. You will always think you need more. He will convince you to test-drive as many people as you can simply because you share a mutual attraction with someone. This is a false perception. We should never believe the lie. God can deliver us from freakish behavioral patterns. Find a prayer warrior, or prayer network who will commit to walking you through your deliverance process. Do not feel embarrassed or ashamed of your addiction. It's real and more prevalent than we think. There are many recovering addicts in our churches today, who are living free from sex addiction. How? 1) Acknowledging the problem. 2) Surrendering the issue to the Lord. 3) Confessing the sin. 4) Renewing your relationship with God.

A WORD FROM THE WISE
You do not want to be known for having sex with multiple people at your church. Being the church floozy is the last thing you want to be remembered for. Many of us have heard of congregations where several church members have been intimate with the same person or each other. Do yourself a favor and take yourself out of that equation. Do not become another victim of closet freak pandemonium. Take your attraction to whoever is the hottest thing on the scene and put it on lock down. It will save you from unnecessary heartache, drama and mayhem.

CLOSET FREAK PROTECTION
Simply because a man attends church does not mean he's risk-free of drama, games, and player tendencies. Don't get me wrong, there is nothing more beautiful than a man in the house of the Lord worshiping God. Nevertheless, you must proceed with caution. In other words, slow down. The last thing you want to do is get wooed by outer appearances and find out you just got hooked up with a closet freak.

For some single believers, church is an open field to meet the opposite sex. Hooking up is their main goal for attending the house of worship. In other words, everybody is not there to experience Jesus Christ. You must be vigilant and sober. Keep your eyes wide open, use discernment and take the time to get to know your special person of interest. You will ultimately save yourself from a potential closet freak encounter.

SIX WAYS YOU CAN DETECT A CLOSET FREAK:

- Calls late at night the majority of time
- Overly interested in your sex-life or lack thereof
- Only wants to meet-up in doors at your house or theirs
- Drops frequent hints about their sexual likes
- Shows little to no interest in settling down
- Enjoys dating multiple people simultaneously

The examples listed are just a few ways you can detect a potential closet freak. Remember, do not rely on outer appearances, however many scriptures a person knows, or how long they've attended church to influence your decision who to spend your time with. The Holy Spirit knows everything about the person you're interested in. If you feel something is not right but you can't quite put your finger on it, then something is more than likely not right. Trust God and keep your dress on. You'll be thankful you did later. *(John 16:13) "However, when He, the Spirit of truth, has come, He will guide you into all truth; for He will not speak on His own authority, but whatever He hears He will speak; and He will tell you things to come."*

7

EMOTIONS

What woman on planet earth doesn't desire sex with security? Most women do. The two are a necessity. One without the other can feel incomplete and unfulfilling, especially from a security point of view. Most women have an innate desire to be held and protected by her mate. It allows us the opportunity to release the weight of the world in a safe and familiar place.

Sex without security can cause feelings of insecurity and fear of the future. Intimacy with a non-husband most often raises an in-depth fear her lover may decide to leave the relationship at any given time. Married women may experience the same fear on some level, especially when she is involved in an unhappy relationship, but single women are at greater risk. Her potential mate has nothing to lose by walking away. He's already single therefore he has no spiritual, ethical or moral incentive to stay.

Women are more prone to become emotionally attached to a man she's having sexual intercourse with in comparison to one she's not. After sex she normally becomes territorial. Thinks about him all day long and feels a strong mental attachment. These factors alone can make her emotions spiral out-of-control. She will often feel as if her lover owes her his heart, time, paycheck, and undying love after the second or third intimate encounter. She later loses all sense of power and control in the situation when her potential mate doesn't fulfill her emotional expectations. In the end, confusion rears its ugly head. She finds herself overwhelmingly frustrated because the relationship is not defined. Is it love or simply sex? She doesn't know.

SEXUAL ATTACHMENT

When a woman's emotions rage with confusion and frustration it is important to understand why. After God created marriage, He said the two shall become one. (*Matthew 19:5*) *"For this reason a man shall leave his father and mother and be joined to his wife, and the two shall become one flesh."* Sexual intercourse is a physical expression of marital unity. An intimate connection can create a powerful bond between a man and a woman even if they haven't taken wedding vows. The emotional state of oneness makes a woman want her sexual partner to treat her with the same love, respect and admiration as if she were his wife. The thought of him cheating with another woman or a man sends her into a frenzy. The problem lies in the fact that he is not her real husband although it feels like it. Therefore confusion and disappointment are knocking on the front door.

A WORD FROM THE WISE

It is not in our nature to habitually engage in sexual intercourse with a man and walk away without feeling a strong tie. Women tend to equate sex and love together as if the two are always in sync. Not so. We can find ourselves in a dangerous situation when we become intimate with a man who considers the relationship purely sexual while we're thinking there is more. It's easy to become head over heels with a potential mate while he's still trying to figure out if he even likes us. Sister, beware of falling in love alone.

KNOW WHAT YOU'RE GETTING INTO

After you've reached a certain age or plateau in life, playing guessing games and wondering if he's in it for the long haul or not can be tiring. It's important to know what river you're swimming in before you dive into the water. Time will be your best friend while discerning your potential mate's motives. Take your time. Slow down and abstain from any sexual contact. Abstinence allows us to think clearly without distractions, overbearing yearnings, and premature expectations.

Sex in marriage is the safest time and setting for intimacy. A single sister won't drive herself crazy trying to figure out if the man loves her or not. She'll know the answer. He's her husband. *(1 Thessalonians 4:3) "For this is the will of God, your sanctification: that you should abstain from sexual immorality; that each of you should know how to possess his own vessel in sanctification an honor, not in passion of lust, like the Gentiles who do not know God."*

FIVE TIPS TO KEEP YOU EMOTIONALLY BALANCED

- Take the time to learn who your man of interest truly is
- Try not to read heavily into every word or gesture
- Find out what his motives are before you invest
- Pray and ask God to show you his heart
- Don't have sex with him or any man before marriage

GOT HOPE?

When life doesn't seem to go our way it's easy to feel a sense of hopelessness. Depression can creep its way into our lives when so many things seem to go wrong all at the same time. To make matters worse, depression isn't addressed as much as it should be in many of our churches. We are encouraged to believe if you love Jesus, you will never feel down or question God. In a perfect world perhaps this is true, but in most cases this theory is unrealistic. We are real people, with real issues. For instance, your finances may be a hot mess. Your boss is working your last nerve and loneliness sneaks its way into your thought life late at night. To top things off you're praying and seeking God for answers, but unfortunately you are unable to hear Him. Your spiritual airwaves are silent, which makes the whole situation seem bleak.

THE BATTLE
Do you sometimes find it hard to smile? Get out of bed? Struggle to visualize the brighter side of life? If you answered "yes" to any of the following questions, then you may be battling an unwanted case of depression. Perhaps you've decided to keep your battle private in order to avoid the risk of being judged or looked down upon by your peers. Maybe you're too ashamed or embarrassed to share your issue with others because of the negative stigmas associated with depression. Although your reason for keeping the issue to yourself is understandable—YOU CAN'T. Satan would love to isolate you and make you believe you're the only one. Trust and believe; you are not alone. Thousands of women are suffering silently in congregations around the country. Why? Fear—fear of what everyone may think. It can keep us mentally frozen and bound up for weeks, months and years if we allow it. Moving beyond this uncomfortable phase is crucial.

First, open up your mouth and ask for help in spite of your preconceived notions of others. No one should fight this battle alone. There are Christian counseling ministries in churches today that are equipped to help you through a difficult season. With a strong support team and consistent prayer depression can be broken. Take your mind back. Your deliverance is one word away.

If you ever feel the need to explore ungodly sources in an attempt to temporarily relieve your pain and anxiety—WAIT. Sex, alcohol, and drugs cannot fix your problem or take away your pain. These damaging outlets can lead you down a deeper whole. When you wake up the next morning the problem is always still there. You'll feel worse than you did before you indulged. Such remedies are designed by the enemy to give you temporary relief that can ultimately destroy you physically, spiritually and emotionally in the end. (1 Peter 5:8) *"Be sober and vigilant; because your adversary the devil walks about like a roaring lion, seeking whom he may devour."* Let the Lord work out whatever is ailing you. He will make a way when you see no way. Your restoration and deliverance are in God alone.

MY STORY: HOPE DEFERRED

In December 2008, I found myself in a vicious battle against depression. It was Christmas time. I was expecting a miracle in my ministry and finances that would change the course of our destiny. After a long season of hearing from God on the matter I firmly believed a breakthrough was soon to come. I was sure God was getting ready to do something great. Suddenly, everything turned for the worse. I lost all of my money in a fundraising effort and found myself thousands of dollars in debt. I became confused and hopeless. "Lord, how could you let this happen? Why am I always going through these challenges alone? I wondered." For several weeks I was unable to hear the voice of the Lord. I felt stuck, believing I was walking through life alone. I rarely got out of bed or talked to anyone on the telephone. I was content rehearsing my problems repeatedly in my mind. Watching television all day was the extent of my daily activities. My house became pity-party central.

Days later, I was forced to make some serious decisions. One of them consisted of closing the doors to our school in Africa. The thought of turning away over one hundred children who sought refuge through our ministry was unbearable. It hurt. "Where was God in all of this? I kept thinking." The enemy was speaking the entire time, telling me, *"You won't make it! Your labor is in vain. Give up! You failed! It's over!"* All of these phrases continued to bombard my mind. I couldn't think straight. Everything looked dark and unfamiliar. My friends were praying, but I still couldn't see any light.

Finally, I called Pastor Malinda, our operations manager at the I CAN FLY School in Kenya. I told him to create a closing strategy for the school and ministry within a week. I sought advice from attorneys here in the United States who could assist in the selling of our building and property in Africa. Days later, Pastor Malinda called back and said, "I'm sorry, Sister, but, I will not forfeit the ministry. If there is no money, so be it. If the staff leaves, let them go. Our God will send us another staff. I will stand until God tells me to stop." My mouth dropped. I was stunned. He wouldn't give up. He ignored my request and continued to believe. I was in awe of God and His ability to move mightily through this man. His faith rendered a small surge of optimism to my hopeless state. "If he has enough faith to hold on then maybe I should too," I thought.

Three months later, I received a call from a former employer. She heard I was still in the United States and thought she'd give me a call. She offered a part-time position at her agency with more pay and fewer hours. Without hesitation, I took the position. I saved each check to pay off the debt I owed. Weeks later, the school staff was getting paid again. The children didn't miss any services offered through the ministry. Although it took one whole year to erase the debt, the Lord made a way through my ex-employer.

● ● ●

I may never understand why the situation turned out the way it did, but God never forgot us. We were not forsaken in a situation that looked dismal and hopeless. He was there the whole time. Even when I didn't see Him, He was there. The times I couldn't hear Him, He was listening. *(Isaiah 44:21) "I have formed you, you are My servant; O Israel, you will not be forgotten by Me!"*

JUST BELIEVE

You have the power to rise up and out of your current situation. You will win this battle. It is not yours to fight in the first place. Let God have it. Take off your boxing gloves and hand over them to the Lord. Reclaim your joy. Tell those suicidal thoughts to go right back where they came from. There is hope and greatness in your future. There is sunshine on the other side of your storm. Don't let the enemy play with your mind. Believe the report of the Lord. Every lie Satan speaks is a deceptive ploy designed to convince you to give up on the destiny and purpose God placed inside of you. *(John 8:44) "When he speaks a lie, he speaks from his own resources, for he is a liar and the father of it."*

SEVEN TIPS TO DEFEAT DEPRESSION

- Read scriptures of God's promises/speak them aloud daily
- Tell your closest friends exactly what you're feeling
- Surround yourself with people who can lift you up in prayer
- Play your favorite praise and worship music
- Dance like you've never danced before
- Do not believe or accept any negative voice in your ear
- Counter every lie with God's word

PIECES

Settling for a piece of a man opposed to all of him is at an all time high. The opinion polls have made it clear. Dating opportunities are decreasing each year and the telephone isn't ringing off the hook like it once was. Moreover, despite the unwanted deficit, we should never settle for less in terms of our bodies, emotions, and spiritual well being. There is nothing wrong with being selfish when it comes to love and intimacy. We all deserve more than a piece of a man. Just imagine; other folks are more than likely taking a piece of Mr. Someone Special also. Where does that leave the single church sister? She is standing in line with the other ladies, waiting to grab a piece of fake love and affection.

PULPIT SEDUCTION
Powerful, God-fearing, attractive men are usually the single church sister's favorite type of guy. He is featured on her secret "America's Most Wanted" list. She is fascinated by his confidence, wisdom, and nurturing spirit. Unfortunately these types of men are few in number in comparison to their female dominated congregations. For this reason alone, our Pastors and church leaders can often become the apple of a single woman's eye.

This kind of attraction has caused hurt and upheaval in many churches today, especially in cases where the man is already married. Why does this happen? The spirit of seduction can wage a war so strong it convinces the single church sister she's got to have him. She'll do whatever is necessary to seduce him. Parading around the offering table with her breasts exposed can often times be the first step toward the goal. In other cases, a sister can dress modestly and exude a humble, quiet, and outwardly subtle demeanor until she gets him alone. She believes fulfilling a piece of her warped fantasy will satisfy her seductive urge. *(Galatians 5:16-17) "Walk in the Spirit, and you shall not fulfill the lust of the flesh. For the flesh lusts against the Spirit and the Spirit against the flesh; and these are contrary to another."*

HALF A MAN SYNDROME
Desperation and the fear of being alone can cause a single sister to settle for second place in a man's heart. She will forfeit her original desire for a healthy relationship for the sake of having a man. Almost any man will do; married, engaged, or otherwise. She believes half a man

is better than nothing. Denial becomes a familiar state of mind. It's easier to pretend the relationship is working instead of recognizing it for what it is—flawed. Although she genuinely desires a monogamous relationship, fragments of attention and sex dispersed on a part-time basis temporarily fulfills her physical need. In the meantime, she's an emotional wreck. Settling for half a man consistently sets her off balance in several ways. Her self-esteem has plummeted. The close relationship she had with God feels fractured. Her peace of mind is now compromised due to her inability to break the hazardous sexual soul tie.

A CHAT ROOM DISCUSSION ON CHEATING

Since 2002 numerous data conducted by experts have reported over 60% of all married men claim to have cheated on their wives at least once. The numbers continue to rise as on-line hook-ups and internet sex steadily replace previous dating methods. In today's society, it's more popular to blame our men for their cheating ways instead of their willing accomplices. Is this a fair observation? No. It takes two to tango. Both parties are equally responsible.

JUST SAY NO

How can we stop infidelity? It's simple. "Just say no." When a single sister says, "no" to a married man, he can no longer cheat on his wife. Furthermore, most single sisters desire a husband of their own. Cheating with someone else's man not only disrupts another woman's family and relationship but it can prolong God's efforts to deliver her future husband. Remember, we serve a God of order.

MARRIED MEN 101

Single sisters should never give themselves the freedom to look at a married man with a slight bit of interest. Once she finds out he's taken—she should run, as well as, snap out of la-la land and put the attraction on lockdown. Forget how fine, muscular or anointed he is. Disregard how much money he's holding in his bank account and ignore what type of 401k he's accruing. Remember—he is married, therefore, he is unable to fulfill a single woman's need for true intimacy and companionship.

Being the other woman is a lonely and depressing place. It is a vicious cycle that builds you up to believe you will one day acquire the whole man with all of the perks. Take note; the other woman never gains the same respect, admiration, and benefits as the wife. The mistress can only play a background role in a married man's production. She must wait on God and believe when the timing is right the Lord will bring her a whole man intended just for her. Her impulsive efforts to fulfill loneliness, desperation and tainted attraction must become a thing of the past. After all, God only wants the best for His daughter. In His eyes she is a jewel. He designed her in His own image; a masterpiece of His divine design.

COOKIE COUPONS

Consider your cookie coupon distribution days officially over. Be honest. You're tired of spreading your cookie around to every man who tickles your fancy. You've been trying to kick the habit for years, but have been unsuccessful. You simply need someone to give you a push in the right direction and tell you the truth. Well, today is your day. Here I am to tell you. You're better than this! There is a man out there that will love you enough to put a ring on it.

Perhaps you've slept with a few men, several men, or so many you can no longer count them on two hands. Remembering all of their names is a struggle. Unfortunately, your frequent sex sample give-a-ways and cookie dough discounts haven't gotten you anywhere except a broken heart, a trip to the abortion clinic, and a major scare with a stubborn sexually transmitted disease (STD) that won't go away. You know the one that a twinge of ointment and a shot of serum won't cure. Sister, the situation may look grim, but don't lose hope, there is still time to turn things around.

At some point in our lives we've all heard our mothers, aunties and grandmother's say, "Baby, don't give away something for nothing." They were right. In the climate of our culture we've become accustomed to sleeping with a man simply because he's cute, we like him, and the sex will probably feel good. We are taking off our dresses to give up the cookie much faster and easier than our mother's and grandmothers did in their day. Yes, they had their issues too. Nevertheless, our standards have plummeted as the years go by. We give it up without hesitation. We're raising the white flag of surrender without a fight. A free seafood dinner, brief chat on-line, and a complimentary whisper in regard to our beautiful breasts and butt size seem to do the trick. Sometimes, obtaining a cookie coupon doesn't require dinner or traditional dating methods. A late night booty call set in motion can spark a full blown love-making fest. No bartering or exchange. Simple, fast, easy and it's over. The cookie was free. Think about it. Our brethren are living on easy street. They don't have to work for it anymore. Cookie nation has become one big amusement park with lots of rides that don't require a ticket and everyone is getting in for free.

COUPON COUNSELING
Distribution habits are hard to break, but it's not too late. There is still time to turn things around. We can

rise above this. Once you set your mind and spirit to change, you can literally alter your life's course. Sharing your body with a non-husband or multiple partners is spiritually and physically unhealthy. God commands we wait upon him to fulfill our sexual desires in Holy matrimony. *(1 Corinthians 6:19) "Or do you not know that your body is the temple of the Holy Spirit who is in you, whom you have from God, and you are not your own?"*

If you're distributing your cookies for financial reasons, you can stop today. Dating someone for the sake of getting the telephone bill, rent or mortgage paid is another form of prostitution. Believing you can't survive without financial assistance from a non-husband is a trick of the enemy. The Lord is your source. You can endure without ungodly assistance. God will see you through. *(2 Samuel 22:31) "As for God, His way is perfect; The word of the Lord is proven; He is a shield to all who trust in Him."*

MY STORY: SPONSORS

While having a friendly conversation with a family friend we began discussing marriage and dating. At the time I had no interest in meeting anyone since I was struggling just to keep all of my business affairs in order. I shared how difficult things had become financially and I wasn't seeing any breakthrough any time soon. After finishing my thought she snapped her fingers as if a light bulb went off in her head. "Oh, girl, you need a sponsor," she said. "Hmmm, I never thought about that. Maybe I'll call a few fortune five hundred companies and see if they'll accept a proposal," I replied. She giggled. "No sweetie, not that type of sponsor. I meant a man who could help you out financially." "Are you serious?" I asked. "Yes, that's how lots of people are getting by now-a-days."

• • •

REALITY CHECK

Getting your bills paid by a generous sponsor will have a hefty price-tag attached. Your donor will expect a pay out. Most times, the sponsorship package will include a coupon exchange in the form of sexual favors, intimacy and spending time together. Although you may be conditioned to believe sponsorship is an acceptable method of survival—it's not. Take yourself out of survival mode and remember who your God is. *(Philippians 4:19) "And my God shall supply all your need according to His riches in glory by Christ Jesus."* The Word of God doesn't say, He'll supply some of your needs, or a few of your needs, but ALL of your needs will be met. Let Him take care of your every concern. Honoring God with your body means more to Him than your rent and telephone bill payments. You're God's chosen. He will see you through every financial battle that arises. You will survive. Put your dress back on and tell your sponsors to lose your telephone number. Trust Him today. Let the Lord be your sponsor. He will provide all of your needs.

CREATIVE SURVIVAL METHODS

- If you live alone, find a roommate and sub-let the space
- Share the bills until you are in a better financial situation
- Reduce your hair and nail appointments
- Find a style that is lower maintenance
- Prepare your meals at home instead of eating out often
- Search for lower cell phone plans that work with your budget
- Tithe to your church/Give offerings to your favorite charity

A FREE PASS

If you've never fully gotten over your ex-husband or your child's father, take a deep breath. It's understandable. He holds a special place in your heart. You may sometimes think you've moved on from the past but your mind often drifts as you reminisce about the good old times you once shared. After all, he was the last person you loved. Every now and then you occasionally have sex with him when you're having a weak moment. The children aren't around and you're feeling in the mood. He was there, you were willing, and you both couldn't help yourselves.

SEX WITH YOUR EX

Is your ex off limits? Most definitely — Yes. The divorce is final. He is no longer your husband therefore the benefits of marriage have been revoked. If your child's father is your weakness, you must put God first. This man is not your husband; therefore he should not reap a cookie coupon harvest. Since a mutual attraction still exists, he is probably hard to resist. To help you through your struggle you must recall why the relationship didn't work out in the first place. Whether it was your fault or his — it's over. The longer you continue offering him cookie coupons, the cycle persists. If you want to be free of your past and stop the emotional roller coaster, let's get off the ride. Once you let go, you can re-build, re-group and heal. Allow God to do a new thing in your life. *(Isaiah 43:18) "Do not remember the former things, nor consider the things of old. Behold, I will do a new thing, now it shall spring forth."*

SUGAR MOMMA

Once upon a time Sugar Daddies were known for showering their women with their every hearts desire. Cars, rent, and clothes—you name it, and a willing sugar daddy would quickly provide it. Although the clean cut, smell good Sugar Daddy still exists, a new phenomenon is on the rise. We call them Sugar Momma's—women who play the role as sponsors for men. Some may refer to them as cougars when a woman is significantly older than her beau although many Sugar Mommas are within the same age range as their mates. For reasons unknown, she finds it necessary to pay all of the bills in the relationship. She mentally struggles to continue her Sugar Momma ways, but she'd prefer to pay the price in order to keep her man close.

Paying a man's bills in exchange for his time, attention, and sexual favors is a fruitless coupon. The relationship is already doomed. The Sugar Momma enables her man to believe he doesn't have to work in order to get her or keep her. He no longer strives to provide for himself since food, shelter, and transportation has already been supplied. Furthermore, a Sugar Momma never truly knows if her man genuinely loves her or not. The financial benefits and cookie coupons can make him happy enough to stay in the relationship regardless of how he feels about his supplier. She will often wonder, "Is he in this relationship because he cares about me, the money or the cookie?

A WORD FROM THE WISE

Take your money and run into the arms of God. He has a better plan for you and your wealth. Being an enabler not only robs you of your self-esteem, but it also makes your lover a dependent. If you desire a healthy relationship with a man, wait on God. With the Lord at the forefront of your union, you will not be tempted to buy love in order to have a man or keep one. Real love is free and it feels right.

THAT'S MY HUSBAND

Have you ever been introduced to an attractive man at your church or on the job and wondered, "Could that be my husband?" When the neighborhood grocery store clerk flirts with you in the check-out line, are you thinking, "Is he my future man?" If you answered yes to the following questions, you have a lot in common with a host of other single church sisters. Any slight attraction to the opposite sex sends us into, "That could be my husband" mode. Counting anyone out is not an option. You never know who could be — The One.

THE WAIT
Most single church sisters have waited their entire lives for God to send them a mate. Some have waited longer than others. Nevertheless, we all know what it feels like to wait. It is uncomfortable and nerve-racking at times. Not knowing the day, the time or the hour in which our desire will manifest can cause anxiety and fear. In the back of our minds we're afraid it may not happen. Why? Years have passed and it hasn't happened yet. We can't tell anyone how anxiously we're waiting for our Boaz to rescue us from the perils of single life. We fear how desperate we may sound to others. Who wants to appear needy and anxious? No one does, but the people closest to us can normally sense the anticipation. They will more than likely quote a scripture when the feeling is strong. *(Philippians 4:6) "Be anxious for nothing, but in everything by prayer and supplication, with thanksgiving, let your requests be made known to God."* And, yes, they are correct. The Bible verse is clear, yet we still find ourselves, thinking—I WANT MY HUSBAND NOW!

FANTASY MAN
Sometimes you can want a husband so bad you begin to fantasize about any man you deem attractive or halfway worthy. Traveling down this road is risky. It can make you appear delusional. After all, the emotional fantasy affair is one dimensional. For instance, assuming your special man of interest is a gentleman, he carries himself as such. He's cordial, treats you with respect when you pass him in the hallway and rushes to open the building door as you enter. You on the other hand, have already visually planned out the wedding.

You've picked out the brides maids dresses, smelled the flowers and rehearsed your wedding vows in the bathroom mirror. You believe there is a chance he'll fall in love with you and pop the big question: Will you marry me? The problem is: You're two hundred feet ahead of the game. You know nothing about him. He could be living a bi-sexual down-low lifestyle or already married.

LESLIE'S STORY: THAT'S MY MAN

Leslie's crush on David was in full motion by the time she found out he was actually married. She decided to do a little research and ask their mutual friends a few questions about his marital relationship. Her friends gave her very little information. Once she and David became closer friends, she asked him point blank. "Are you happily married?" He claimed the marriage was an unhappy one. Leslie was more than satisfied with his response. The gloomy marriage reply was just enough to give her hope for the future. The chemistry they shared proved he had to be The One in her eyes. Weeks later, the adulterous affair was in full motion. They met once a week at a local motel.

Finally, several months had passed. Leslie could no longer hide the relationship from her family and friends. She often referred to him as her husband. She claimed the already married man as her own. She felt strongly this man was ordained by God to be her husband. She could feel it. Nonetheless, years passed and the delusional bond grew stronger. In the meantime, David stayed married to his wife. Leslie remained faithful in the relationship. She spent countless hours convincing others God had sent her a mate who was already married. One day, her world came crashing down when David divorced his wife of fifteen years and married a different woman. Sadly, Leslie spent the next few years trying to figure out what she did wrong.

● ● ●

DISCREET DECEPTION
The human mind and Satan's tricks are a bad combination. Deception is the enemy's greatest tool in his effort to deceive and destroy us. He targets our most intimate vulnerability and works it to his advantage. If you're not aware a possible scheme against you is in full motion, you just might fall for it and wake up not knowing what hit you. During times and seasons of vulnerability its crucial to stay prayed up and study the Word of God. Your spiritual antennas will work better. You'll be able to spot a trick before it can fully draw you in. *(Matthew 24:4) "And Jesus answered and said to them: Take heed that no one deceives you."* The enemy knows we are emotional creatures. He is skilled at using your natural desires and periodic frustrations in his plan to create a psychological attack. Your ability to detect this hideous assault on your mind will save you from a lifetime of heartbreak.

A WORD FROM THE WISE
Proceed with caution before assuming someone is your husband, especially if you're the only person that heard it. The circumstances are very different if your unmarried boyfriend heard it too. In this instance, the both of you can ask God for confirmation and move forward. Moreover, if you're the only one that heard a certain

gentleman is your husband, slow down and wait. Ask the Lord for clarity and guidance. Remember, we serve a God of order. If the relationship is out of order, it's more than likely not God. The Lord will not send you a husband who is already married to someone else. *(1Corinthians 14:40) "Let all things be done decently and in order."* When you feel confused and grieved in your spirit about who your husband is or is not, hand the situation over to God. Let Him sort out the confusion and clutter in your mind. You will drive yourself crazy trying to figure out the details of your future. Pray and ask God to put a hedge of protection around you. Seek the Lord like never before and ask Him for peace.

MR. PROPHECY

MY STORY: A WORD FROM GOD OR MAN?
Over the years I've had the privilege of meeting some of the most powerful and sincere believers of our time. Many would often ask, "Why aren't you married?" I wish I knew the answer, but for the sake of avoiding a long drawn out conversation about my personal life, I would answer, "God's timing." One day, one of my curious colleagues pulled me to the side of the room and said, "Sister Givens, I see your husband. Yes, the Lord showed him to me. He's tall with wavy hair and you two have a ministry together. He's on the way." I was excited for the first few months, expecting a tall, wavy haired gentleman to surface at one of the events I attended or perhaps I'd meet him on a flight. Unfor-

tunately, years passed with no interest from any of my tall, wavy haired male friends. Not even one stranger who fit that description approached me.

Years later, a prayer warrior stopped me on the way home from a meeting. She knew I was leaving the country soon and approached me with a prophecy. "You're getting ready to marry an African man on your next trip. Get ready!" She stated. Four months later, I sat in the Nairobi International airport waiting for an outbound flight back to Los Angeles. I was more confused than ever. My alleged African husband never surfaced after living on the continent for three and a half months. My mind raced. All of the prophecies concerning my future husband were different and fruitless. These were powerful people of God. "Who missed it?" I wondered. I found myself tangled up into one big prophetic ball of confusion. Birthed from my own desire to be married, I became mentally consumed. Where is the mystery man I longed to meet? Finally, after years of toiling with the possibility of meeting Mr. Prophecy, I became tired and weary. Exhausted from wondering who Mr. Prophecy really is…

● ● ●

A WORD FROM THE WISE

Are you vigorously trying to figure out who your future husband is based on a prophecy? If you answered yes to this question, do yourself a favor and stop now. I could share over a dozen prophecies with you I've been told over the years, but I won't. I will spare you the burden. It would drive you crazy like it almost drove me crazy. Trying to figure out who Mr. Prophecy is can be emotionally draining. Your lack of peace concerning the issue can also disrupt other areas in your life. Free yourself. Let it go. Mr. Prophecy will appear at the appointed time. Not our time, but God's timing. The Lord knows exactly who he his, where he is, and when he's supposed to show up. Remember, we serve a God of peace not confusion and bondage. (*1 Corinthians 14:33) "For God is not the author of confusion but of peace, as in all the churches of the saints."*

We all genuinely want to receive a personal relationship prophecy with open arms. Why? Each prophetic utterance normally brings a sense of relief and comfort. A mustard seed of hope can make a world of difference when you're battling loneliness. Nevertheless, we must be discerning and sober. There are many hurting women in our churches today because of a misguided prophecy that left them confused and disappointed.

PROPHELYING

If you attend a church that moves in the gifts of the Spirit you've probably already received a word of knowledge, exhortation or prophecy. Interestingly, many church-goers can unknowingly practice their prophetic agenda without weighing the costs of offering false hope and expectations. So, sisters, be careful. Every prophecy is not from God. There are many sincere believers who will attempt to prophesy, but speak from their own genuine concern for you or their personal opinion. Do not allow the shortcomings of others to trip you up. Be graceful. Thank the person who delivered the word and release it to God after spoken. Do not hold on to it with anxiousness. Let God be God.

TIME IS NOT A FACTOR
Watching the time clock can be frustrating, especially when you're rehearsing a prophecy repetitively in your mind. Once we receive a prophetic word we tend to expect the full manifestation of it within the confines of our own time constraints. This is a human occurrence. In the Lord's eyes time is not a factor. The Almighty is timeless. If the prophecy regarding your love-life is true, God will handle it. Free yourself of anxiety. Walk in the truth and favor that is upon you. He will do exactly what He said He would do. *(Numbers 23:19) "God is not a man, that He should lie, nor a son of man, that He should repent. Has He said, and will He not do? Or has He spoken, and will He not make it good?"*

PROPHETIC TRUTHS
Living a balanced life after receiving a prophecy is essential to your emotional wellbeing. When your husband appears the Lord will make it clear. Having peace and joy are critical while awaiting the revelation of God's divine will. Several women who have received true prophecies concerning their mates are currently living happily ever after. You will too. For now, take one step at a time. Trust God and continue living for today. The Lord has your life in His hands.

A PRAYER
Lord, you know my future. You have every detail concerning my life in the palm of your hand. I release this prophecy to you today and ask that Your will be done in my personal life. Give me peace when I feel anxious and confused. Give me hope when I doubt that you are able to manage my life. Take control, oh God. Manifest everything you have ordained for my life in your divine time. In the name of Jesus Christ, I pray. AMEN!

14

WHEN YOUR MAN IS THE DEVIL

He's finer than the well-built trainer at your local gym. Style, poise, and personality are all in place. Everything seems perfect. You're digging him and he's returning all the love. He calls when he says he will and tells you how beautiful you are on a consistent basis. You've been swept off your feet and you don't think you want to come down. Why would you? You haven't felt this high on love in a long time. This man is exactly what you've been waiting for. There's just one problem. He's not who he says he is. Mr. Wrong sent a representative to fill in for him the first ninety days of your relationship. By the time you realize something is not quite right with your new man, you're in too deep. You've invested your time, money and emotions. You even offered him the cookie. You can feel it in your spirit. This relationship is all wrong, but the thought of leaving him seems unbearable. In order to cope with your decision to stay, you slip into a state of denial. You convinced yourself the relationship is not so bad after all. Months later, you woke up one morning and realized you don't even recognize yourself anymore. You've been seduced by a counterfeit.

A GOD SEND

A man of God will always enhance your life. Not take away. He lifts you up, encourages you, and gives you a peaceful feeling down on the inside. Your relationship is balanced, not unstable and confusing all of the time. He resembles a blessing not a curse. God's man is a gift. You're grateful for him when you're in his presence. You don't worry or fret about your future. You both can feel God in your midst. Your lives make sense when you're together. You smile without effort. He makes you proud. There is peace. It's good, its right, its God.

TOXIC RELATIONSHIPS

A man that draws you away from God was not sent by Him. There may have been a time in your life when you put God before everything. The Lord was always first, but since the arrival of Mr. Wrong, nothing has been the same. You rarely attend church like you once did. You'd prefer to keep your new man at a distance from your family and friends. Why? They can easily detect a counterfeit. In the meantime, you struggle with the fact that you love two men, but one of them can literally destroy you.

The enemy is clever. He will tempt you with a representative that tickles your fancy just enough to let him in the back door. Satan knows exactly what you like, how you like it, and the best wrapping paper to package him in. Sister, if a man was not sent by God then who do you think led him your way? The devil. A man dispatched by the enemy will rarely support your faith, desire to abstain from sex until marriage, or your Godly ambitions. This trap was set to make you fall. These events do not always happen over a short time span. It can take several months to recognize the scheme in full bloom. The representative will always stay for a decent period of time until it becomes tired. Some people can put up a facade for weeks, months, and even years.

The gift of discernment is crucial. The Lord will reveal exactly who your new man is. If your discernment is off or underdeveloped, you will think the representative is the real thing. Remember, he will do and say all the right things at the right time. Just think; you can find yourself in bed, making love to a counterfeit. Sounds scary? It is. Pray, pray, pray and ask God who this man really is when he knocks at your door. Before you allow yourself to become smitten by Mr. Wrong, watch and listen.

VICTIM NO MORE
Domestic abuse is on the rise. Many single sisters have found themselves enslaved to a hazardous relation-

ship they once believed to be a blessing. Continuous yelling, cursing, name-calling and, BOOM, she gets knocked out. Our sister completely lost consciousness. Now, she's trying to figure out how she got there and how to get out. Why does this happen? For a few reasons: 1) Her relationship is in an advanced phase and she is afraid to leave. 2) She is financially dependent on her abuser. 3) They spend countless hours together therefore she doesn't know what she would do without him. 4) She has no clue how to escape the abusive situation. She is alone and emotionally attached. 5) Her self-esteem is low.

HELP IS ON THE WAY

Your days of victimization can be over with one word. "Help!" Do not remain silent any longer. There are people in your local area who are willing and waiting to assist you. Yes, this may sound easier said than done, but you must remember who your God is. The Lord is able to deliver you out of a difficult situation when you see no way out. *(2 Timothy 4:18) "And the Lord will deliver me from every evil work and preserve me for His heavenly kingdom."*

Pray and ask the Lord to protect you. Be honest with Him about your fear and hesitation. Be open to assistance. Take the first step. Ask Him to guide you to a person or place of refuge. He will do it. It's not too late to start over. A new beginning is within your reach. Do not allow the enemy to rob anymore days, hours or years of your precious life. You are God's daughter. Believe it, and walk in your authority. You can make it. You are a survivor. You shall live. *(1 Corinthians 15:1) "But thanks be to God, who gives us the victory through our Lord Jesus Christ."*

SIX WAYS TO KNOW YOUR MATE IS WRONG FOR YOU

- Pulls you away from God instead of draws you closer
- You've gone backwards in life rather than forward
- Does not respect your faith, spiritual morals and beliefs
- You've experienced very little peace since you met
- You are physically, mentally or sexually abused
- Attacks your self-esteem regularly without reservation

*Please note: This list is not intended to fully determine your mate's spiritual arrival status. Moreover, it can be used as a simple guide to help you recognize their role in your life. In an effort to find the truth, please pray, watch and listen to what God has to say.

WOLF ALERT

Hook-ups between single sisters and men of the cloth are happening more often than we think. Single sisters have become a playground for promiscuity in select churches around the country. The reports are staggering. Our laundry is dirty. Yes, filthy. Moreover, we can clean up our houses—the big ones and little ones. There is still time. One little word can turn everything around. Sisters, we have the power to say, "No!" You can protect yourselves from the wolves in sheep's clothing who seek to devour you.

SECRET AFFAIRS

An affair with your church leader is out of order. Do not allow social status, prestige or a subtle case of coercion to persuade you otherwise. It doesn't matter what story you are told in an attempt to justify a sexual advance. Your shepherd's Godly position consists of protecting the sheep (you), feeding the sheep (you) and guiding the sheep (you) toward the high calling of God. *(John 10:11) "I am the good shepherd. The good shepherd gives His life for the sheep."* Where does sexing you up factor into the shepherd and sheep relationship? It doesn't. Unfortunately, your leader is a closet freak who preys on vulnerable women in the congregation. Why? It's convenient and we've remained silent.

We each have an innate sense of right and wrong. If a particular situation feels wrong, it probably is wrong. The Holy Spirit will push your red or yellow button as a warning signal in times of need. If your pastor or church leader comes on to you by flirting, touching you, or looking you up and down as if you were a buttermilk biscuit, do not minimize it as an innocent occurrence. Most seducing spirits begin their conquests in a quiet, non-threatening manner. These subtle advances are expressed to gauge how far you're willing to go. If an encounter with your leader seems slightly inappropriate, stay as far away as you can. Trust the warning signal. You will avoid becoming the next victim of closet freak pandemonium.

MY STORY: PASTOR WOLF & HIS SHEEP

Several years ago I had the opportunity to link up with a smaller congregation across town. I was impressed with the Pastor the first time we met. He was knowledgeable of the Word, young, handsome, and often expressed his desire to elevate himself in the things of God. Shortly after, we became friends. Being a perceptive woman, I noticed the women in his congregation were obviously smitten by him. He had charisma and style. He seemed like the perfect package.

The closer our friendship grew the Lord began to reveal disturbing details of the future. I woke up one Tuesday morning and the Holy Spirit had spoken: "Tell him to go to those two women and fix it." Although I didn't fully understand the message and the magnitude of it, I obeyed. I called him immediately at seven-thirty in the morning. He claimed he had no idea what I was talking about. As his friend and confidant I expressed my willingness to support him and help sort out the issue with these unknown women. He continued to deny any problem existed. My spirit was vexed. Everything inside of me shouted, "A big mess was on the horizon." I could feel it. Two weeks later, a teenage girl came forward and admitted she was having sex with the Pastor. Two additional under-aged girls were named in the scandal but one of them denied any relationship with him. After the deacons questioned all parties involved and the parents were notified, he continued to deny any wrong doing. Two of the girls felt shattered and betrayed by his overt denial of their relationship. One of them lost her virginity to the Pastor.

The congregation and ministry team leaders suffered for a little while. A few Sundays later after the scandal died down, the church continued with business as usual. The Pastor remained in his position and preached his heart out like he had any other Sunday. Two of the teenage girls left the church. One stayed. She was in love with him.

● ● ●

If your faith has been damaged by a wolf in sheep's clothing, take your eyes off the perpetrator. The Lord is a vindicator. Turn your attention back to Him. He is a redeemer and a healer. Release your hurt, pain and disappointment at the feet of the Lord. Suffer no more. Man is imperfect. We fall, we sin, and hurt people because of our own issues and insecurities. Do not allow mans discretions to hinder your faith in God. Tell the Lord exactly how you feel and release your past. You are God's chosen. It's His desire to prosper you and give you a future full of promise and success. Do not allow wolves to rob you of your destiny in God because of unforgivingness. This too shall pass. God will heal your heart. *(Jeremiah 33:6) "Behold, I will bring it health and healing; I will heal them and reveal to them the abundance of peace and truth."*

A WORD FROM THE WISE

If a church leader tries to seduce you by initiating a sexual advance, tell someone and run as far away as you can. Do not feel ashamed or embarrassed to yell, "Wolf Alert!" Remember, this is not your burden to carry. You are not the perpetrator in this situation. Break the silence and stop this vicious cycle. You will save yourself and another victim from unnecessary suffering. The pain and disappointment our sisters and brothers are carrying from wolf abuse can be diminished with a word. Let's rise up.

FOUR WAYS TO DETECT A POTENTIAL WOLF

- Enjoys sharing their sexual history
- Keeps your relationship a secret from church members
- Flirts with you when their spouse is not around
- Finds ways to get you alone by yourselves

DIRT & BONES

Most single church sisters stroll through the double doors of the church on Sunday looking confident, fashionable, and ready for the world. No one knows she's carrying an invisible suitcase. Her luggage is filled to the rim with unresolved issues, dirt, and bones that weigh her down. She claps, sings and dances in the center aisle for several minutes until the music stops. It felt good. The Pastor preached. The sermon was encouraging. She's feeling emotionally empowered, but for how long? A couple of days at best, but when the Pastor delivered the altar call, she couldn't move. Her feet were stuck to the candy apple red carpet underneath the pews. Too many people were watching. Unloading her suitcase in front of a crowd of curious eyes was unthinkable. Any twinkling of exposure would be devastating. She'd rather take her dirt and bones to the grave than risk someone knowing her uncomfortable truth. So, she leaves feeling good for a little while, but no real change has taken place. Where does she go from here? No where. The cycle begins again—starting next Sunday.

The reality of exposing the contents inside our suitcases is scary. "What will everyone think if they found out who I really am?" you wonder. You don't believe church people can handle your issues. After all, no one speaks candidly about the challenges you're facing. Like an elephant in the room, there are clearly others battling the same temptations, but you dare not speak it aloud. The price of exposure seems much too hefty. If anyone knew your dark secret, you risk feeling ashamed and ostracized by others. So, instead of releasing the weight that holds you hostage, you tightly embrace your dirt and bones.

THE UGLY TRUTH

Are you in bondage to an ugly secret or habit you're too ashamed to tell? If so, the enemy gets a thrill watching you sit and suffer in the exact same condition you were in last year. It's his way of holding you hostage to whatever you did or are currently involved in. Sister, do not give Satan that kind of power. Confessing your issue or sin to God is the most liberating thing you can do. Do not allow yourself to remain a slave to your emotions and guilt. Once you confess the sin, you are no longer responsible for it. *(Micah 7:19) "He will again have compassion on us, and will subdue our iniquities. You will cast all our sins into the depths of the sea."*

It doesn't matter how foul you may believe your situation is, you cannot stop God from loving you. Your abortion(s), suicidal thoughts, reckless behavior, pole dancing, and sexually transmitted diseases (STD's) will not make Him love you any less. Whatever your issues are, it's still not enough to stop His love. He cares for you too much to leave you where you are.

At the end of the day we all have a past. Most of us did not join our various churches with a clean slate. Our unspoken issues range from child molestation, incest, physical abuse to daddy issues. The after affects of these heinous crimes have resulted in the need for unhealthy intimacy and our reluctance to leave toxic relationships. Until our issues have been acknowledged and addressed, we will remain victims of damaged emotions. The days of keeping our skeletons in the closet must cease. Our bones are killing us.

NOBODY KNOWS

Not a single person on the face of the earth may know your dirt, but God does. He can take it and make a masterpiece out of it. You must first allow God to use it. He will create something beautiful. Dirt can only grow a harvest after a seed has been planted. Allow the Lord to plant a seed of hope and healing on the inside of you. Take every heartbreaking thing that has happened in your life and release it. Ask the Lord to use it and grow a harvest that can change and deliver the next sister. Trust Him with your dirt and those bones you're tightly holding onto. It's time to let go of the past and grow into the beautiful flower God intended.

SPIRITUAL DETOXIFICATION

Like anyone trying to break a bad habit or turn down their favorite junk food item, detoxification can feel uncomfortable and new. This physical cleansing process prompts your body to release everything old, unhealthy and toxic that has lain dormant inside your body. Interestingly, toxic waste has been known to cause disease, sickness and even death. Most physical detoxification methods are designed to make you healthier, stronger and function with more energy.

God's cleansing methods are similar. In this case, a spiritual renewal is the goal. The requirements are clear: Repent and turn away from every unhealthy sexual relationship that hinders your spiritual progress. (*Acts 17:30*) *"Truly, these times of ignorance God overlooked, but now commands all men every where to repent."* God is there, waiting for you to return back to your first love—Him. The Lord never left you. He is waiting in great anticipation for you to come on home.

CUTTING LOOSE

If you're struggling with the decision to end a sexual relationship(s), it is clearly understandable. Your desire to remain with the person you're having sex with is normal due to the attachment theory. Spiritual detoxification is uncomfortable and painful, which is why we wish to avoid it. Detachment from your lover is much like cutting out your heart without anesthesia. Why? Sex with a non-husband creates a soul tie and emotional attachment as if the couple is actually already married, but in the eyes of God they are not.

Sexual intimacy creates a bond like no other. For women, cutting the tie is extremely difficult because our emotions usually escalate during the love-making process. Detaching oneself from a partner(s) can be even more complicated when a long term relationship was involved. Being physically and emotionally attached to a man for several months or years can be costly. The tie is always stronger when you've shared a great deal of time, emotional energy, and bonding with your respective families and friends.

TIES THAT BIND

Have you ever wondered why you'd rather close your eyes and die than break up with your partner? It's simple. This indescribable bond between two lovers is no longer physical. It reigns deeper than our human level of understanding, which is why the Word of God tells us, sex should only be shared between married couples. *(Matthew 19:5) "For this reason a man shall leave his father and mother and be joined to his wife, and the two shall become one flesh."*

God understood the degree of bonding two people would share can feel unbreakable, which is one of the reasons why our traditional wedding vows include, till death do us part. For some single church sisters, it can take several months or even years to recover from a severed sexual relationship. Moreover, God's healing power is real. If we repent and turn away, the Lord will heal our hearts and set us back on the path He originally ordained for our lives. Will you miss your ex-lover and all of the treats that accompanied him? Yes, for a while, but, once you've set your mind and spirit to change in your pursuit of God's will for your life, the pain will surely decrease. Your sexual blinders will disappear. You will soon thank God He led you out of Egypt and back to the Promise Land where His divine will for your life resides.

INVISIBLE LINES

Boundaries are relevant and necessary if you aspire to keep your classy little dress on. Setting up a list of guidelines you commit to follow is imperative to your overall success. Such guidelines are designed to keep you out of harms way while dating or pursuing a serious relationship with a potential mate. Remember; we all have weaknesses. Knowing exactly what our weaknesses are and being real with ourselves about them is crucial. For example, if ice cream makes you feel warm and fuzzy all over, I suggest you don't ask your man to drive you down to the local ice cream shop at ten o'clock at night for a cone of rainbow sherbert. This is not a wise idea since ice cream makes your mind wander places it shouldn't go.

MY STORY: MOVIE NIGHT

I love watching movies, but there are only certain films I can view these days. One night, after perusing a chain of cable news channels, I found an interesting story on a popular station. I was hooked on the story line immediately. Within minutes the characters were in the midst of a steamy love scene. I continued to watch thinking the scene would end shortly. Well, it didn't. The love scene continued for minutes. I was mentally drawn in and couldn't turn the dial. The scene became fascinating. My mind reverted back to the days of cookie mania. Finally, the steamy scene ended. I began thinking of all the things my life was missing. Remembering how great it was to be held, kissed and caressed resurfaced. I was mad at myself. I should've changed the channel while I had the chance, but I didn't. I actually craved for more.

I fell asleep that night and dreamed of all sorts of situations I hadn't thought about in a long time. I enjoyed reminiscing. It was the closest I could get to the real thing. So I let myself indulge in the fantasy of being intimate with a man again. My thoughts had turned into feelings I wanted to literally fulfill. I couldn't think of one ex-boyfriend I could conveniently contact. They were all married, engaged, or hooked up in some way or another. Finally, I snapped out of it. I was forced to shake myself and come back to earth. I prayed, "Lord, please remove these images from my mind before I do something I'll regret."

● ● ●

AVOIDING TRIGGER HAPPINESS

A trigger can be an aroma, a song, an item, or a person, place or thing that reminds you of sex and foreplay. Once you've identified all of your triggers you can set your list of guidelines accordingly. I've heard many women refer to the sweet smell of an ex-boyfriend's cologne as a trigger. After inhaling that exact aroma or one similar, the mind reverted back to an intimate rendezvous with MR. WRONG. The brain is a powerful tool. It can take us places we'd rather not go or thought we forgot. Try your best to keep your mind focused on things that are positive and serene. *(Isaiah 26: 3) "You will keep him in perfect peace, whose mind is stayed on You because he trusts in You."*

WORDS OF THE WISE

Think of every possible trigger that presses your "go" button. Make a note of it and plan your strategy, especially if you are currently dating or desire to do so. You may even plan to limit any physical interaction with your potential mate. Some single church sisters feel comfortable hugging, kissing and embracing the man their dating. Moreover, if any of these actions work as a trigger, you may want to reconsider including them in your dating activities. It only takes one touch to send you over the edge. Let's be real: You know the spot. For others, the right squeeze can potentially take you to a place of no return.

STAYING ON COURSE

Your invisible lines will help keep you on track, especially if you're an ex-cookie coupon distributor or a recovering closet freak. You will love yourself later for avoiding the triggers. We must take extra precaution not to place ourselves in compromising situations. Thank God for coffee shops. The new latte and cappuccino coffee trend makes it easier to meet up, chat and share without the temptation to take your conversation into the bedroom. A public setting is always safe. Your dress is guaranteed to stay on.

BEFORE "I DO"

For single church sisters, sex outside of marriage can take a mental and physical toll. The ramifications of pre-marital sex can be extreme. The morning after can be devastating. A sexually transmitted disease, unplanned pregnancy or a one night stand that ends with an unreturned phone call is heart breaking. Risking our health, dignity and relationship with God is not worth a hit and run encounter or a series of sexual escapades with a man who has no plans to make us his wife. We must protect ourselves. The only full proof method to avoid a major catastrophe is abstinence. Yes, it is easier said than done, but something has got to change. We can no longer do this to ourselves. Let's remember God's plan. His design is always best. Don't forget He created sex — Sex in marriage.

Intimacy in marriage will give you the full experience of romantic bliss. The Bible speaks of romance in a profound way that is more exciting than any daytime soap opera. The scriptures written in the Song of Solomon address intimacy in a way that clearly depicts a marital relationship filled with intense love, sex, and romance. Let's wait on God. His plan for love and intimacy is better than anything we could imagine.

FOUR STEPS TO CREATING YOUR INVISIBLE LINES

- Identify each trigger
- Create a set of do's and dont's based on your list
- Share your guidelines with accountability partners
- Make your guidelines a necessity

IS THE FAT LADY SINGING?

At this point in your life you're probably wondering, "Lord, where is my husband?" Many years have passed and you're still single. You've been faithful to God, read the Word and serve in the church. You've been obedient to God's commands, yet no one has asked you out on a date or even offered to buy you a cup of coffee. You cannot figure out, what is going on. For those of you who have been asked out for a night on the town, you may have become frustrated with the corn flakes, closet freaks, counterfeits, and wolves in sheep's clothing that cannot seem to lose your telephone number. You might be asking, "When is the real thing finally going to come along?"

Lord knows, I wish I could tell you where your soulmate lies in wait, but unfortunately, I don't have the answer. One thing is for sure. God knows every detail of your life — past, present, and future. *(Jeremiah 29:11) "For I know the thoughts that I think toward you, says the Lord, thoughts of peace and not of evil, to give you a future and a hope."* He has the, who, what, why, when, and where, parts of your life already pieced together. The psychics are not privy to this information, so do yourself a favor and stop calling them for an update on your single status. Our God is all knowing and all powerful. Your age, financial status, or past does not prevent Him from performing His perfect will in your life. The Lord has your every concern under control although it doesn't feel that way at times.

THE REAL DEAL

Let's face it! You're tired of waiting. Your hormones are raging out of control. Keeping your sex drive under submission is a battle in itself. It's lonely showing up to the company Christmas party alone each year. And furthermore, another "when are you getting married" question just might send you over the edge. Sister, you are not alone. These feelings are common and understandable, but in spite of your thoughts, do not lose heart. The possibility of meeting God's special someone is not over. I'm sure you've heard the statement: It Ain't Over Until the Fat Lady Sings! This announcement may be applicable for others, but you have the power to determine whether she sings or not. Only God can decide how your story ends. Remember, He is the only one with the power to shut down the rivers of hope. If He has not told you to stop believing, then don't. Tell the fat lady to go home. She can't perform unless you put her on your program. Trust God in spite of your periodic frustration. *(Proverbs 3:5) "Trust in the Lord with all your heart, and lean not on your own understanding."*

MY STORY: SOMEONE TO CALL ME MOMMY

A family member once suggested I go ahead and have sex with a man just to get pregnant. "That's desperate and out of order" I thought. I was irritated by the mere idea. I wasn't thinking about having children or wanting any at the time--well not until my diagnosis. Painful cramps, long periods and heavy bleeding were always an issue since I was twelve year old. I would always brace myself for the worst when that time of the month came. I walked around for several years thinking my extreme case of heavy bleeding and rushing through dozens of mattress sized maxi-pads in a week was normal. One day my period didn't seem so common after all. A blood clot the size of my fist released itself when I went to the bathroom. I knew something was wrong. I didn't know what to do. I had no health insurance.

Three days had gone by. My heavy flow continued for two whole weeks. I began to feel weak and disoriented. Getting out of bed every morning and moving around the house was a challenge. I finally broke down and told my mother I'd been bleeding for two weeks straight. She demanded we find a doctor. I called a few low cost clinics in the yellow pages and one of them agreed to meet immediately. My mother drove. By the time we arrived I passed out on the hospital floor. My blood count had plummeted down to a three-point-five. The normal count was twelve. The doctor reported I was suffering from uterine fibroids. I had no clue what a fibroid was. "Cancer?" "No, fibroids, the doctor said." He suggested I have them removed by a surgical procedure called a mayomectomy. The process would eliminate the fibroid and leave my uterus fully intact. "Will I be able to have children?" I asked. "Yes, unless there is a problem during the surgery and we need to perform a hysterectomy." I gasped. I was very familiar with the term. The doctor suggested I take a deep breath and think about it. He later recommended I should plan on having a baby within six months after the mayomectomy procedure if I chose the surgery option. He said it would be best for the sake of my health and the future child.

My mind raced. Surgery! Fibroid! Baby! No husband! What was I going to do? I was confused. I thought of every ex-boyfriend in my database. Maybe I could call one of them and tell him the situation and he'd take care of me. Perhaps he'd want to get married and go ahead and have a baby. I was sure my family and closest friends would understand. All of these thoughts, plans and ideas consumed my very being. I was driving myself crazy. I so badly wanted a child now. The thought of not experiencing a taste of motherhood was frightening. To hear a child call me "Mommy" would be a delight. Time was running out. I became frantic. For the first time ever, I longed to be a mother. Finally, I had to stop and pray. I prayed and asked God to remove the desire. There was no man and no baby plans. Only a grapefruit sized fibroid growing on top of my uterus. "What is God's plan in this situation? I wondered." There was no answer—only silence. Reading the Bible, praying and staying close to the women who regularly encouraged me was pivotal. "God is not done. He has the final word, keep praying," My sister friends repeatedly said. So, I did. This time I prayed differently. I included the words "Lord, let Your will be done" at the end of my prayer requests. I worshiped more. I praised Him more and I could feel a breakthrough. The Lord had it all under control.

• • •

TICK TOCK TICK

Having sex with a man just to get pregnant is not in God's divine plan. The Lord is working out every detail of your life in this season. Your biological time clock may be ticking, but I encourage you to continue honoring God with your body and feminine desires. When we attempt to fix our own lives out of desperation and fear, we are bound to create a mess. Slow down, take a deep breath and remember who your God is. If children are a part of His divine will for your life, He will make a way. We cannot put God in a box. Be open. Children come in all sorts of packages.

OPTIONS

Biological children are indeed a blessing from God. Moreover, do not forget other options exist, such as infant adoption and foster adoption. Today, single women are building their families in non-traditional ways. Although these methods may not be the way you imagined having children, allow God to bless you in a manner you never expected. There could be a child who needs a mother exactly like you to nurture them.

If you feel called to be a mother and sense in your spirit the Lord may have an adoption plan in store for you, consider yourself a blessed woman. Pray and ask the Lord to lead and guide your steps through the adoption process. There may be a child in your local community who is abandoned. Perhaps the Lord has chosen you to bring healing and hope to the baby. You should research adoption agencies and local Family Service Centers that specialize in adoption and foster care. Remember, you don't have to invite the fat lady to sing at your program. It's not over!

MY STORY: THE OFFERING

After seven years of toiling with the fibroid issue I received good news. My grapefruit sized fibroid shrank down to the size of a peanut. A strict diet of fruits and vegetables, low sugar, no beef or pork and a Chinese herb a friend told me about paid off. The nurses and doctor were stunned. My periods were stable again. Three days a week, with little cramping, and a light flow. I'd forgotten what it felt like to be completely normal again. I couldn't thank God enough.

Soon after, the thought of having children resurfaced. It would've been nice to conceive a little boy. My mind drifted again. "I have a few good years left to have a son," I thought. Reality quickly set in. There was no man in my life and I didn't have a clue when or if he'd show up. So, instead of throwing myself a pity party I decided to give the Lord an offering. I closed my eyes and touched my lower abdomen. I dedicated my womb back to God, and said:

"Lord, you created my body. I thank you for preserving my womb. Since my body is yours and this womb belongs to you, I offer it back to you. Do as you please with it. If you choose to birth a child through me, I'll praise you. If you choose not to bring a child in this world through this vessel, I'll still praise you. In the name of Jesus Christ, AMEN!"

My longing and hurt ended that night. My uterus and childbearing woes could no longer hold me hostage. I offered them back to God. It was time to look forward. If a child remains a part of God's great plan for my life, it will happen at the appointed time. Nothing and no one will be able to stop it—not even me.

● ● ●

THE GOD OF TIMING

We all have a tendency to force our personal expectations on God. We expect Him to show up and perform miracles simply because we said so. Our finite minds are fixed on the notion that He should do things our way. We know best, right? Not so. The Lord knows exactly what we need and when we need it. Time does not make Him nervous. We are the worried ones. We live according to a clock. God lives in eternity therefore He is not governed by time. The God of Timing is fully aware of our biological time clocks and human expectations. *(Isaiah 55:8) "For my thoughts are not your thoughts, nor are your ways My ways, says the Lord."*

If we desire peace of mind, we must trust God in spite of how we feel and what we see. Through the rocky roads of our disappointments we must rely upon Him.

In the midst of our delayed dreams and false starts we must believe He has a plan. I know your life doesn't seem to make sense at times, but trust Him any way. He will not let you fall. *(1Peter 5:7) "Cast all your cares upon Him, for He cares for you."*

OPEN UP

Live each day to the fullest. Open yourself up to the unexpected and embrace positive change. Do not focus on what you're lacking in this season. Spend time and energy cherishing all of the wonderful blessings you do have. Be spontaneous. Save your money and take a trip to a tropical island with your favorite sister friends. Better yet, book a flight to Africa, Asia or Eastern Europe and visit an orphanage. Make a child smile you've never met before. Be open to new friendships and relationships with people who don't look like you. Relinquish your fear of dating a man of another race and background. Explore different foods, art and cultures. Step outside of your box of familiarity and let God be God. He can show you a brand new way of living, so you won't remain overwhelmed with your present circumstances. Remember, you have options. The fat lady cannot sing at your program unless YOU invite her…

A DREAM

Calling all visionaries, dreamers, and goal-getters to the floor. If that's you, stand up. Sisters, we are more powerful than we think. We serve a mighty God that is able to accomplish unimaginable works in our lives. *(Ephesians 3: 20) "Now to Him who is able to do exceedingly abundantly above all that we ask or think, according to the power that works in us."*

The dream God created for your life has the power and potential to change the world around us. Our dreams and visions can positively affect one person, dozens, hundreds and even millions. You'll know when the vision is from God — it's bigger than you. You may not possess the skills, raw talent and resources to accomplish it, but God does. The Lord planted the dream down on the inside of you because He knew He could trust you with it. You would be the one to protect and nurture it. You'll hold your head up high while others laugh, mocking you for believing in something that hasn't fully manifested. *(Joel 2: 28) "And it shall come to pass afterward that I will pour out My Spirit on all flesh; your sons and your daughters shall prophesy; your old men shall dream dreams, your young men shall see visions."*

WHY ME?

Your personal and spiritual gifts were designed to place you in a position of purpose and power. God intends to use everything you personally and spiritually possess to manifest His divine will for your life and others. Your life has purpose and reason. You were born with a divine assignment already in place. *(Jeremiah 1:5)"Before I formed you in the womb I knew you; Before you were born I sanctified you; I ordained you a prophet to the nations."* Running or hiding from the purpose and plan for your life will return void. Your reason for being will always be there. Embrace it. Allow the Lord to order your steps in regards to the next level of your purpose.

STAY ON THE PATH

Have you ever wondered why the Lord always pulls you out of a mess when you're repulsively caught up? It's called purpose. He can only allow us to wallow in a pigpen for so long. The enemy will attempt to keep you stuck in the mud by creating distractions and temptations deliberately designed to take you off course. Satan recognizes the power and potential that lies in you.

It could damage his fruitless scheme. Doubt, fear, and low self-esteem are his most frequent weapons. If you succumb to the trick, the dream may be delayed. Nevertheless, the Lord is faithful. He will redeem you and position you once again for purpose.

MY STORY: BUTTERFLIES

Nothing has been the same since 2001. I took my first missions trip to Kenya, East Africa. It was the year I said, "Yes" to the vision. I was standing on top of a steep, dusty hill in a remote village one hour east of Nairobi. Suddenly, a dream-like picture showing several buildings standing on the mountain was placed before me. They were scattered throughout the barren land. I was in awe of what I had seen. I gasped for air and cleared my throat. I looked up into the blue and white cotton candy figured clouds and asked, "Lord what are trying to tell me?" I heard His voice clearly, "YOU WILL BUILD!" I almost passed out. "Me? Build? I can't. Find someone else. I'm not qualified. I'm broke. I'm too young. I'm a woman. Send a man, I replied." The mission seemed too large.

Finally, after three days of grappling with the assignment, I surrendered. Weeks later, an adult literacy program was opened for twelve eager women who were unable to read and write. Within three years, the program grew from twelve to three hundred women who traveled for miles on foot to receive the education. Within one year of our expansion two pre-schools were opened and the first building was complete. In 2008 we established the first High School in the area. Within months of the High School expansion, the Butterfly Project planning process began. Rescuing child brides, victims of female genital mutilation, and HIV/AIDS orphans became our cause. Building a home for the girls is a dream that burns in the depths of my spirit. The Butterfly House, I call it, is a place of refuge, healing and transformation for vulnerable girls who feel forgotten. You see, the dream expanded.

● ● ●

CHOSEN FOR A PURPOSE
God didn't make a mistake when He chose you to carry a dream. It doesn't matter if you're blessed with five dollars or five million in your bank account. Single, divorced, or widowed. It doesn't matter. You were chosen for a divine purpose. Although all of the pieces to your vision may not have manifested yet, it's crucial you stand on what you know to be true. Do not be moved by what you see in the natural realm. God will supply the pieces to the puzzle as you remain faithful on the journey. Do not look to the left or the right. Keep your eyes on Jesus. The Lord knows exactly what He's doing. He is working things out on your behalf. He is paving the way before you.

A WORD FROM THE WISE
Embracing the dream will help you stay out of harms way. Feeling needy and overwhelmingly frustrated will no longer dominate your existence. Of course, we are all human with real desires, emotions, and physical needs that God created. Nevertheless, with clear focus on God and His divine assignment, you can find a sense of balance in your state of singleness. The dream will make you feel alive. Go forth, Sister. Dream big and kick doubt and fear to the curb.

SEVEN TIPS TO FOLLOW ON A DREAMERS JOURNEY

- Write the vision down and make it clear (Habakkuk 2:2-3)
- Set an action plan in motion with specific goals
- Post the vision in a safe place where you can see it
- Give yourself specific target dates to complete tasks
- Ask the Lord to order your steps as you pray
- Ask Him to reveal your divine assignment in this season
- Stay focused and trust God no matter what

I AM

MY STORY: MY LIFE

Like every little girl who dreams of her wedding day, I did also: Bright yellow tulips were plastered on the end of each pew. Tall white candles streamed the center aisle. The preacher was standing in the pulpit ready to begin. The flower girls were dressed in gold and white Cinderella outfits, holding the hand of my five-year old nephew, indiscreetly picking in his nose as they walked toward the crowd. The church was filled to capacity and it was the happiest day ever. I was getting married.

Can you believe it? I artistically crafted each wedding feature in my mind throughout the years. I'd sometimes imagine being whisked away in a white carriage after the reception with a handsome man who loved me more than life. I had it all planned out. I presumed these events would take place before my twenty-fifth birthday. My husband and I would have two children, a boy and a girl. Our daughter would look exactly like me. As far as I was concerned, this was a for sure route to happiness. For a few sisters in my circle the fairytale became a reality. They married before age thirty, settled down in beautiful homes and raised a family with a man they called husband.

After attending several weddings I was sure my turn was next. But one year passed, then another, and another. I was the one in the crowd whose life took a different turn. I couldn't understand why I was still single. I've always been a logical person. I believed everything in life should make sense. From what type of car I drive, to which neighborhood I live in, and why I am in my late-thirties with no children. It wasn't until an encounter with the Spirit of I AM occurred, everything changed, even my struggle.

● ● ●

THE VISITATION

When the Spirit of I AM visitation took place I experienced the overwhelming presence of God. There were no words, no sounds. He simply breathed into the atmosphere. I couldn't move. I stood in awe of Him. His presence engulfed my very being. Tears rolled down my face. The sweet smell of God's breath was greater than anything I'd encountered in the past. I was intoxicated by His splendor. Within an instant, all of my issues, questions, complaints and "why me" moments disappeared. I felt free. A new level of trust was birthed. My worries, thoughts, and ideologies regarding my future seemed less consuming. I could breathe knowing whatever I face will all work together for the good. Do I still desire intimacy? Yes, I do, but for the first time in a long time, I found peace and balance. I no longer allow the feeling of being held by a man to overwhelm my mind and daily activities. I firmly believe when the time is right God will perform His perfect will in each of our lives. Worrying about it, holding on to it, and allowing our fantasies to control our thought lives is too emotionally taxing. God has a plan much greater than our limited expectations. His vision vastly supercedes anything we could do on our own. As we wait, continue to trust Him. Our lives are in His hands.

BE ENCOURAGED

Arise, woman of God. Mount up on wings like an eagle. Soar above every weight and affliction. Take hold of who you are and whose you are. You are the daughter of the Most High. Embrace your royalty. Remember who your God is and settle no more. Be bold. Be fearless. He is greater than your single status, ruler over loneliness, the healer of your disappointments, and the forgiver of our transgressions. *(Psalm 34:17) "The righteous cry out, and the Lord hears and delivers them out of all their troubles."* He is the Great I AM.
(Exodus 3:14) "And God said to Moses, "I AM WHO I AM." And He said, "Thus you shall say to the children of Israel, "I AM sent me to you."

I AM your provider
I AM your strength
I AM your healer
I AM your deliverer
I AM your broken heart fixer
I AM your comforter
I AM the great I AM

Thirst no more daughter….. I AM

Books by Sha' Givens

═══════════════════════════

THROUGH THE STORM
(Fiction)

I AM WOMAN:
Walking In God's Divine Purpose
(Non-Fiction)